Monthly Expense STARTING POINT

INCOME £5,600   **EXPENSES** 2286   **DIFFERENCE** 3314

HOUSING EXPENSES

RENT/~~MORTGAGE~~ £1215

TAXES Council 130

TOTAL 1345

TRANSPORTATION COSTS

CAR PAYMENT 284

INSURANCE

GAS/petrol 60

TOTAL 344

MEDICAL & DENTAL EXPENSES

MEDICATION

TOTAL 20

OTHER EXPENSES

CREDIT CARD

CREDIT CARD

TOTAL

UTILITIES & HOUSEHOLD BILLS

GAS 30

ELECTRIC 30

WATER 33

AF378753

INTERNET/CABLE 24

SUBSCRIPTIONS 11

PHONE 24

TOTAL 152

FOOD & GROCERY

GROCERY 200

DINING OUT 50

TOTAL 250

PERSONAL EXPENSES

CLOTHING 50

ENTERTAIMENT 100

OTHER 25 swimming

OTHER

OTHER

TOTAL 175

TOTAL MONTHLY EXPENSES

2286

Financial GOALS

GOAL	AMOUNT	BY WHEN
Trip to Australia	5000	September
Trip to Spain	1000	April
Trip to Spain	1000	

Congratulation on committing to gaining control of your finances!

The best place to start is at the beginning. The first thing you'll do is write down all your sources of income and all your expenses. This will give you your starting point.

Next, write down your financial goals. Maybe you want to save to buy a house, or pay off a credit card, or start giving to charity. Write down everything you want to do over the coming year so you can start planning how to make that happen.

Next, are the payment trackers. These are used to track monthly payments so you never forget a payment, as well as to record amounts of payments so you can see when you paid extra versus just making the minimum payment which is motivation to keep pushing toward your goals.

Next, you'll find a variety of saving trackers you can mix and match whether you prefer to just track amounts, or you prefer to color in your progress on a gauge for visual encouragement of all the progress you are making.

Next, you'll find a variety of debt trackers to encourage you as you make payments on time and get closer to your goals. There are a variety of styles to choose from to mix and match, from simple numbers to charts to color to see your progress.

Next, you'll see a set of 12 undated monthly trackers so you can start your goals any time during the year. There is a 2-page monthly calendar to write down due dates, goals, or reminders for each month. Each month also has a budget overview so you know what to expect for the month and can plan ahead. There are also five weekly trackers for each month to track all income and expenses to gauge your progress. This helps you see where you may need to make adjustments to your expenses based on what you actually spend.

At the end of the 12 months is an end-of-the-year monthly recap to see what your monthly income and expenses look like after taking control of your finances for a year.

2020 Year At-A-Glance

January

S	M	T	W	T	F	S
			1	2	3	4
5	6	7	8	9	10	11
12	13	14	15	16	17	18
19	20	21	22	23	24	25
26	27	28	29	30	31	

February

S	M	T	W	T	F	S
						1
2	3	4	5	6	7	8
9	10	11	12	13	14	15
16	17	18	19	20	21	22
23	24	25	26	27	28	29

March

S	M	T	W	T	F	S
1	2	3	4	5	6	7
8	9	10	11	12	13	14
15	16	17	18	19	20	21
22	23	24	25	26	27	28
29	30	31				

April

S	M	T	W	T	F	S
			1	2	3	4
5	6	7	8	9	10	11
12	13	14	15	16	17	18
19	20	21	22	23	24	25
26	27	28	29	30		

May

S	M	T	W	T	F	S
					1	2
3	4	5	6	7	8	9
10	11	12	13	14	15	16
17	18	19	20	21	22	23
24	25	26	27	28	29	30
31						

June

S	M	T	W	T	F	S
	1	2	3	4	5	6
7	8	9	10	11	12	13
14	15	16	17	18	19	20
21	22	23	24	25	26	27
28	29	30				

July

S	M	T	W	T	F	S
			1	2	3	4
5	6	7	8	9	10	11
12	13	14	15	16	17	18
19	20	21	22	23	24	25
26	27	28	29	30	31	

August

S	M	T	W	T	F	S
						1
2	3	4	5	6	7	8
9	10	11	12	13	14	15
16	17	18	19	20	21	22
23	24	25	26	27	28	29
30	31					

September

S	M	T	W	T	F	S
		1	2	3	4	5
6	7	8	9	10	11	12
13	14	15	16	17	18	19
20	21	22	23	24	25	26
27	28	29	30			

October

S	M	T	W	T	F	S
				1	2	3
4	5	6	7	8	9	10
11	12	13	14	15	16	17
18	19	20	21	22	23	24
25	26	27	28	29	30	31

November

S	M	T	W	T	F	S
1	2	3	4	5	6	7
8	9	10	11	12	13	14
15	16	17	18	19	20	21
22	23	24	25	26	27	28
29	30					

December

S	M	T	W	T	F	S
		1	2	3	4	5
6	7	8	9	10	11	12
13	14	15	16	17	18	19
20	21	22	23	24	25	26
27	28	29	30	31		

Payment **TRACKERS**

Use your payment trackers for a variety of reasons:

If you have goals of paying off debt in a specific period of time, divide the total amount to pay off by the number of months to get the approximate amount you need to pay each month to achieve your goal. You'll need to add the monthly interest to the total payment to meet your goal. You can also find payoff calculators online to help with this which take the interest payments into consideration for you.

The yearly tracker will help you make sure you don't accidently miss a payment.

The dept payment trackers can be used to keep an eye on the amounts you are paying when you are trying to pay off debt early.

Yearly Bill TRACKER

YEAR:

DESCRIPTION	AMOUNT	DUE	JAN	FEB	MAR	APR	MAY	JUN	JUL	AUG	SEP	OCT	NOV	DEC

NOTES

Debt Payment TRACKER

Debt: _______________   **Creditor:** _______________   **Date:** _______________

Starting Balance: _______________   **Account:** _______________

JAN	FEB	MAR	APR	MAY	JUN

JUL	AUG	SEP	OCT	NOV	DEC

Closing Balance: _______________

Debt: _______________   **Creditor:** _______________   **Date:** _______________

Starting Balance: _______________   **Account:** _______________

JAN	FEB	MAR	APR	MAY	JUN

JUL	AUG	SEP	OCT	NOV	DEC

Closing Balance: _______________

NOTES

Debt Payment TRACKER

Debt: ______________ **Creditor:** ______________ **Date:** ______________

Starting Balance: ____________ **Account:** ____________

JAN	FEB	MAR	APR	MAY	JUN

JUL	AUG	SEP	OCT	NOV	DEC

Closing Balance: ____________

Debt: ______________ **Creditor:** ______________ **Date:** ______________

Starting Balance: ____________ **Account:** ____________

JAN	FEB	MAR	APR	MAY	JUN

JUL	AUG	SEP	OCT	NOV	DEC

Closing Balance: ____________

NOTES

Debt Payment TRACKER

Debt: ___________________ **Creditor:** ___________________ **Date:** ___________________

Starting Balance: [ ] **Account:** [ ]

JAN	FEB	MAR	APR	MAY	JUN

JUL	AUG	SEP	OCT	NOV	DEC

Closing Balance: [ ]

Debt: ___________________ **Creditor:** ___________________ **Date:** ___________________

Starting Balance: [ ] **Account:** [ ]

JAN	FEB	MAR	APR	MAY	JUN

JUL	AUG	SEP	OCT	NOV	DEC

Closing Balance: [ ]

NOTES

Debt Payment TRACKER

Debt: _______________ **Creditor:** _______________ **Date:** _______________

Starting Balance: [   ] **Account:** [   ]

JAN	FEB	MAR	APR	MAY	JUN

JUL	AUG	SEP	OCT	NOV	DEC

Closing Balance: [   ]

Debt: _______________ **Creditor:** _______________ **Date:** _______________

Starting Balance: [   ] **Account:** [   ]

JAN	FEB	MAR	APR	MAY	JUN

JUL	AUG	SEP	OCT	NOV	DEC

Closing Balance: [   ]

NOTES

Debt Payment TRACKER

Debt: _______________ **Creditor:** _______________ **Date:** _______________

Starting Balance: _______________ **Account:** _______________

JAN	FEB	MAR	APR	MAY	JUN

JUL	AUG	SEP	OCT	NOV	DEC

Closing Balance: _______________

Debt: _______________ **Creditor:** _______________ **Date:** _______________

Starting Balance: _______________ **Account:** _______________

JAN	FEB	MAR	APR	MAY	JUN

JUL	AUG	SEP	OCT	NOV	DEC

Closing Balance: _______________

NOTES

Savings TRACKERS

Use your savings trackers for a variety of reasons:

If you have goals of saving for something special, use one of the trackers to see that savings add up and get excited about the progress you are making.

There are a variety of methods to track your saving amount to cater to your personal preference.

Use them to color in as you save more and more toward your goal and get excited seeing the color fill in the tracker sheet.

Use the gauges to color in like a thermometer as your savings grow.

If you like to see the numbers, use the tracker charts to write the amounts you save and when you put that money away, so you don't forget to keep adding to your savings efforts.

I've included pages with specific savings goals such as saving for a house or a vacation, and some without specific goals so you can write your own in.

Vacation **SAVINGS**

Total: $ ______________    **: $** ______________

Holiday SAVINGS

Total: $ ____________   : $ ____________

Savings TRACKER

SAVINGS GOAL

END DATE

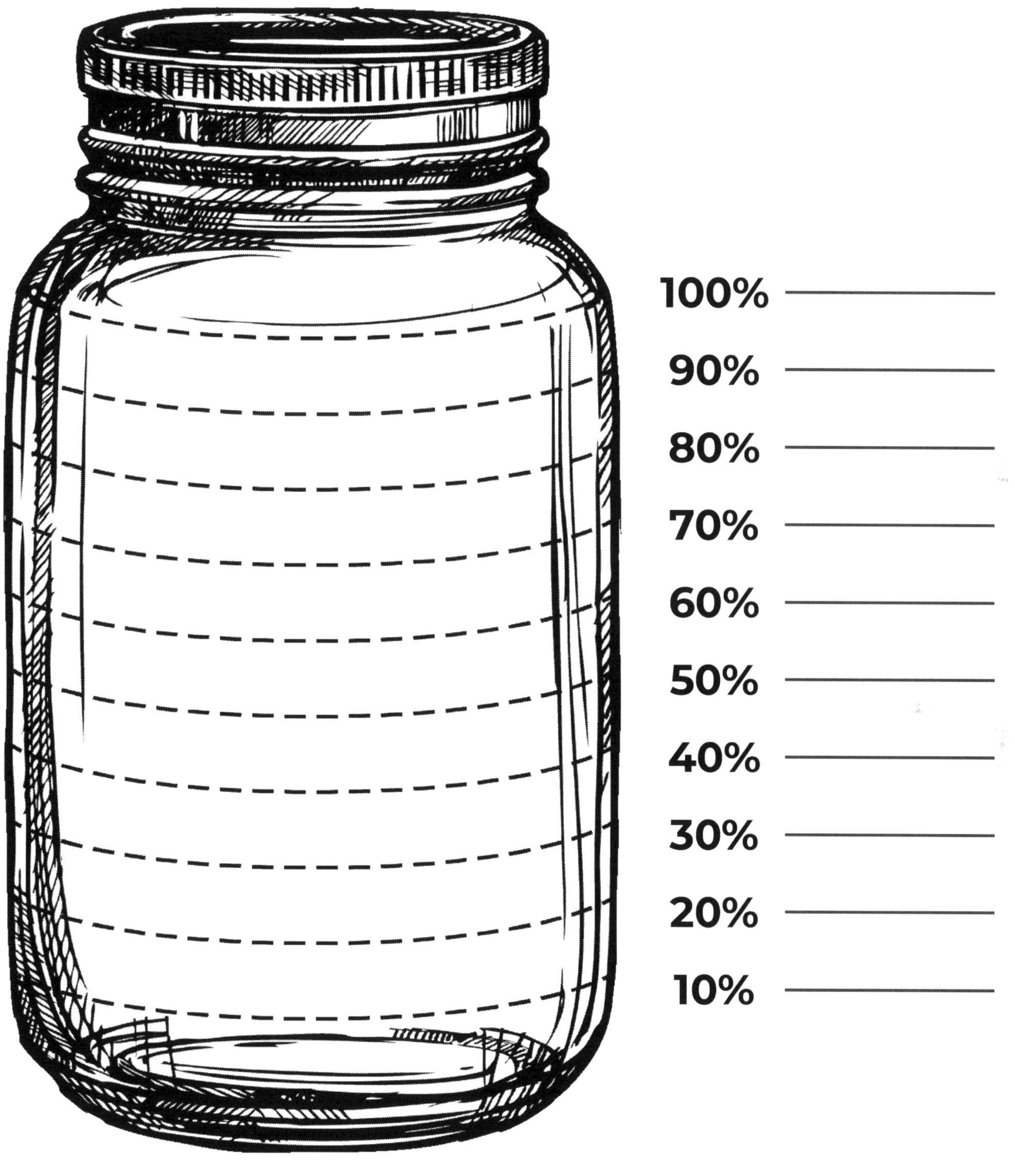

100%

90%

80%

70%

60%

50%

40%

30%

20%

10%

MONEY SAVING IDEAS

My House FUND

Enter your total savings goal at the bottom of the thermometer. This is the amount you need to purchase your home. Then, every time you manage to add money to your house fund, color in the graphic!

MY HOUSE FUND TRACKER

100%

90%

80%

70%

60%

50%

40%

30%

20%

10%

0%

$
$
$
$
$
$
$
$
$
$
$
$
$
$
$
$
$
$
$
$
$

NOTES & MILESTONES

Every dollar counts!

My Car FUND

Enter your total savings goal at the bottom of the thermometer. This is the amount you need to purchase your car. Then, every time you manage to add money to your car fund, color in the graphic!

NOTES & MILESTONES

Every dollar counts!

My Vacation FUND

MY CAR FUND TRACKER

Enter your total savings goal at the bottom of the thermometer. This is the amount you need to book your vacation. Then, every time you manage to add money to your vacation fund, color in the graphic!

100%

90%

80%

70%

60%

50%

40%

30%

20%

10%

0%

$
$
$
$
$
$
$
$
$
$
$
$
$
$
$
$
$
$
$
$

NOTES & MILESTONES

Every dollar counts!

FUND

Enter your total savings goal at the bottom of the thermometer. This is the amount you need to reach your goal. Then, every time you manage to add money to your fund, color in the graphic!

NOTES & MILESTONES

100%

90%

80%

70%

60%

50%

40%

30%

20%

10%

0%

$
$
$
$
$
$
$
$
$
$
$
$
$
$
$
$
$
$
$
$
$

Every dollar counts!

FUND

Enter your total savings goal at the bottom of the thermometer. This is the amount you need to reach your goal. Then, every time you manage to add money to your fund, color in the graphic!

100%

90%

80%

70%

60%

50%

40%

30%

20%

10%

0%

$
$
$
$
$
$
$
$
$
$
$
$
$
$
$
$
$
$
$
$
$

NOTES & MILESTONES

Every dollar counts!

Savings CHART

ITEM I AM SAVING FOR	COST	TIME FRAME

MONEY TRACKER	DATE	SAVED	BALANCE

100%

75%

50%

25%

NOTES

Savings CHART

ITEM I AM SAVING FOR	COST	TIME FRAME

MONEY TRACKER

100%
75%
50%
25%

NOTES

DATE	SAVED	BALANCE

Savings **CHART**

ITEM I AM SAVING FOR	COST	TIME FRAME

MONEY TRACKER	DATE	SAVED	BALANCE

100%

75%

50%

25%

NOTES

Savings **CHART**

ITEM I AM SAVING FOR	COST	TIME FRAME

MONEY TRACKER		DATE	SAVED	BALANCE

MONEY TRACKER

100%

75%

50%

25%

NOTES

Savings **CHART**

ITEM I AM SAVING FOR	COST	TIME FRAME

MONEY TRACKER	DATE	SAVED	BALANCE

100%

75%

50%

25%

NOTES

Debt TRACKERS

Use your debt trackers for a variety of reasons:

If you have goals of paying off debt, use one of the trackers to see your progress and get excited about the shrinking balances.

There are a variety of methods to track your debt payoff to cater to your personal preference.

Use them to color in as you pay more and more toward your goal and get excited seeing the color fill in the tracker sheet.

Use the gauges to color in like a thermometer as your debt shrinks.

If you like to see the numbers, use the tracker charts to write the amounts you pay down and when the payments were made, so you don't forget to keep whittling away at your debt.

I've included pages with specific debt payoff goals such as paying off a car loan or credit card, and some without specific goals so you can write your own in.

Mortgage PAYOFF!

Total: $ _______   🏠: $ _______

Car Loan PAYOFF!

Total: $ _______   : $ _______________

Car Loan PAYOFF!

Total: $ _________   : $ _____________

Credit Card PAYOFF!

Total: $ _______   : $ _______________

Credit Card PAYOFF!

Total: $ __________   : $ __________________

Credit Card PAYOFF!

Total: $ ⬚ : $ ______________

PAYOFF!

Total: $ ☆ : $ _______________

PAYOFF!

Total: $ ☆ : $ ________________

PAYOFF!

Total: $

☆ **: $** ______________

Credit OVERVIEW

ACCOUNT	DUE DATE	MINIMUM DUE

CREDIT LIMIT	INTEREST RATE	CREDITOR

STARTING AMOUNT	TARGET PAYOFF DAY	ADDITIONAL INFORMATION

DATE	PAYMENT	BALANCE	NOTES

Credit **OVERVIEW**

ACCOUNT	DUE DATE	MINIMUM DUE

CREDIT LIMIT	INTEREST RATE	CREDITOR

STARTING AMOUNT	TARGET PAYOFF DAY	ADDITIONAL INFORMATION

DATE	PAYMENT	BALANCE	NOTES

Credit OVERVIEW

ACCOUNT	DUE DATE	MINIMUM DUE

CREDIT LIMIT	INTEREST RATE	CREDITOR

STARTING AMOUNT	TARGET PAYOFF DAY	ADDITIONAL INFORMATION

DATE	PAYMENT	BALANCE	NOTES

Credit OVERVIEW

ACCOUNT	DUE DATE	MINIMUM DUE

CREDIT LIMIT	INTEREST RATE	CREDITOR

STARTING AMOUNT	TARGET PAYOFF DAY	ADDITIONAL INFORMATION

DATE	PAYMENT	BALANCE	NOTES

Credit **OVERVIEW**

ACCOUNT	DUE DATE	MINIMUM DUE

CREDIT LIMIT	INTEREST RATE	CREDITOR

STARTING AMOUNT	TARGET PAYOFF DAY	ADDITIONAL INFORMATION

DATE	PAYMENT	BALANCE	NOTES

Monthly **TRACKERS**

The monthly trackers make it easy to stay on track to achieve all your financial goals.

Start with the undated 2-page calendars for each month so you can start whenever you want. There's plenty of space to write due dates or reminders to stay on track with your financial goals.

Each month you'll fill out the budget overview so you know how much money you expect to come in, and how much you expect to go out. This helps you understand what might be left over for something fun or extra money to put toward your goals. It also helps you make adjustments to expenses or raise additional funds during months you may have more expenses than income.

The weekly progress trackers are a place to write down everything you spend each week to locate those sneaky places where you spend more than you might think you do, then make adjustments.

There are five weekly progress trackers for each month so you have space for both four week months and five week months.

At the end of the month, add up all your income and expenses from each week to compare to your budget and gauge your progress. This part is important because it helps you make adjustments as sometimes life happens.

In no time at all you'll more progress than you ever dreamed you could and be well on your way to crushing all your financial goals!

MONDAY	TUESDAY	WEDNESDAY	THURSDAY

MONTH AT A GLANCE

FRIDAY	SATURDAY	SUNDAY	NOTES

Budget **OVERVIEW**

UTILITIES	BUDGET	SPENT

PERSONAL	BUDGET	SPENT

HOME	BUDGET	SPENT

TRASPORTATION	BUDGET	SPENT

FOOD / DRINKS	BUDGET	SPENT

MEDICAL	BUDGET	SPENT

GIVING	BUDGET	SPENT

DEBTS	BUDGET	SPENT

INCOME	AMOUNT	DATE

OTHER	BUDGET	SPENT

Weekly **PROGRESS**

WEEK OF

	GOAL	ACTUAL	DIFFERENCE + / -
EARNED			
SPENT			
SAVED			
DEBT			

INCOME	AMOUNT
BUDGET:	TOTAL:

SAVED	AMOUNT
BUDGET:	TOTAL:

EXPENSES	AMOUNT
BUDGET:	TOTAL:

Weekly **PROGRESS**

WEEK OF

	GOAL	ACTUAL	DIFFERENCE + / -
EARNED			
SPENT			
SAVED			
DEBT			

INCOME	AMOUNT
BUDGET:	TOTAL:

SAVED	AMOUNT
BUDGET:	TOTAL:

EXPENSES	AMOUNT
BUDGET:	TOTAL:

Weekly **PROGRESS**

	WEEK OF

	GOAL	ACTUAL	DIFFERENCE + / -
EARNED			
SPENT			
SAVED			
DEBT			

INCOME	AMOUNT
BUDGET:	**TOTAL:**

SAVED	AMOUNT
BUDGET:	**TOTAL:**

EXPENSES	AMOUNT
BUDGET:	**TOTAL:**

Weekly **PROGRESS**

WEEK OF

	GOAL	ACTUAL	DIFFERENCE + / -
EARNED			
SPENT			
SAVED			
DEBT			

INCOME	AMOUNT
BUDGET:	TOTAL:

SAVED	AMOUNT
BUDGET:	TOTAL:

EXPENSES	AMOUNT
BUDGET:	TOTAL:

Weekly **PROGRESS**

	WEEK OF

	GOAL	ACTUAL	DIFFERENCE + / -
EARNED			
SPENT			
SAVED			
DEBT			

INCOME	AMOUNT	EXPENSES	AMOUNT
BUDGET:	TOTAL:		

SAVED	AMOUNT		
BUDGET:	TOTAL:	BUDGET:	TOTAL:

MONDAY	TUESDAY	WEDNESDAY	THURSDAY

FRIDAY	SATURDAY	SUNDAY	NOTES

Budget OVERVIEW

UTILITIES	BUDGET	SPENT

PERSONAL	BUDGET	SPENT

HOME	BUDGET	SPENT

TRASPORTATION	BUDGET	SPENT

FOOD / DRINKS	BUDGET	SPENT

MEDICAL	BUDGET	SPENT

GIVING	BUDGET	SPENT

DEBTS	BUDGET	SPENT

INCOME	AMOUNT	DATE

OTHER	START	FINISH

Weekly **PROGRESS**

WEEK OF

	GOAL	ACTUAL	DIFFERENCE + / -
EARNED			
SPENT			
SAVED			
DEBT			

INCOME	AMOUNT
BUDGET:	**TOTAL:**

SAVED	AMOUNT
BUDGET:	**TOTAL:**

EXPENSES	AMOUNT
BUDGET:	**TOTAL:**

Weekly **PROGRESS**

WEEK OF

	GOAL	ACTUAL	DIFFERENCE + / -
EARNED			
SPENT			
SAVED			
DEBT			

INCOME	AMOUNT
BUDGET:	TOTAL:

EXPENSES	AMOUNT
BUDGET:	TOTAL:

SAVED	AMOUNT
BUDGET:	TOTAL:

Weekly PROGRESS

WEEK OF

	GOAL	ACTUAL	DIFFERENCE + / -
EARNED			
SPENT			
SAVED			
DEBT			

INCOME	AMOUNT
BUDGET:	TOTAL:

SAVED	AMOUNT
BUDGET:	TOTAL:

EXPENSES	AMOUNT
BUDGET:	TOTAL:

Weekly PROGRESS

WEEK OF

	GOAL	ACTUAL	DIFFERENCE + / -
EARNED			
SPENT			
SAVED			
DEBT			

INCOME	AMOUNT
BUDGET:	**TOTAL:**

SAVED	AMOUNT
BUDGET:	**TOTAL:**

EXPENSES	AMOUNT
BUDGET:	**TOTAL:**

Weekly **PROGRESS**

WEEK OF

	GOAL	ACTUAL	DIFFERENCE + / -
EARNED			
SPENT			
SAVED			
DEBT			

INCOME	AMOUNT

BUDGET: TOTAL:

SAVED	AMOUNT

BUDGET: TOTAL:

EXPENSES	AMOUNT

BUDGET: TOTAL:

MONDAY	TUESDAY	WEDNESDAY	THURSDAY

FRIDAY	SATURDAY	SUNDAY	NOTES

Budget OVERVIEW

MONTH

UTILITIES	BUDGET	SPENT

PERSONAL	BUDGET	SPENT

HOME	BUDGET	SPENT

TRASPORTATION	BUDGET	SPENT

FOOD / DRINKS	BUDGET	SPENT

MEDICAL	BUDGET	SPENT

GIVING	BUDGET	SPENT

DEBTS	BUDGET	SPENT

INCOME	AMOUNT	DATE

OTHER	START	FINISH

Weekly PROGRESS

WEEK OF

	GOAL	ACTUAL	DIFFERENCE + / -
EARNED			
SPENT:			
SAVED			
DEBT			

INCOME	AMOUNT	EXPENSES	AMOUNT

BUDGET: TOTAL:

SAVED	AMOUNT

BUDGET: TOTAL:

BUDGET: TOTAL:

Weekly PROGRESS

WEEK OF

	GOAL	ACTUAL	DIFFERENCE + / -
EARNED			
SPENT			
SAVED			
DEBT			

INCOME	AMOUNT
BUDGET:	**TOTAL:**

EXPENSES	AMOUNT
BUDGET:	**TOTAL:**

SAVED	AMOUNT
BUDGET:	**TOTAL:**

Weekly **PROGRESS**

WEEK OF

	GOAL	ACTUAL	DIFFERENCE + / -
EARNED			
SPENT			
SAVED			
DEBT			

INCOME	AMOUNT
BUDGET:	**TOTAL:**

SAVED	AMOUNT
BUDGET:	**TOTAL:**

EXPENSES	AMOUNT
BUDGET:	**TOTAL:**

WEEK OF

	GOAL	ACTUAL	DIFFERENCE + / -
EARNED			
SPENT			
SAVED			
DEBT			

INCOME	AMOUNT
BUDGET:	TOTAL:

SAVED	AMOUNT
BUDGET:	TOTAL:

EXPENSES	AMOUNT
BUDGET:	TOTAL:

Weekly PROGRESS

WEEK OF

	GOAL	ACTUAL	DIFFERENCE + / -
EARNED			
SPENT			
SAVED			
DEBT			

INCOME	AMOUNT
BUDGET:	TOTAL:

SAVED	AMOUNT
BUDGET:	TOTAL:

EXPENSES	AMOUNT
BUDGET:	TOTAL:

MONDAY	TUESDAY	WEDNESDAY	THURSDAY

FRIDAY	SATURDAY	SUNDAY	NOTES

Budget OVERVIEW

MONTH

UTILITIES	BUDGET	SPENT

PERSONAL	BUDGET	SPENT

HOME	BUDGET	SPENT

TRASPORTATION	BUDGET	SPENT

FOOD / DRINKS	BUDGET	SPENT

MEDICAL	BUDGET	SPENT

GIVING	BUDGET	SPENT

DEBTS	BUDGET	SPENT

INCOME	AMOUNT	DATE

OTHER	START	FINISH

Weekly PROGRESS

WEEK OF

	GOAL	ACTUAL	DIFFERENCE + / -
EARNED			
SPENT			
SAVED			
DEBT			

INCOME	AMOUNT
BUDGET:	TOTAL:

SAVED	AMOUNT
BUDGET:	TOTAL:

EXPENSES	AMOUNT
BUDGET:	TOTAL:

Weekly PROGRESS

	GOAL	ACTUAL	DIFFERENCE + / -
EARNED			
SPENT			
SAVED			
DEBT			

INCOME	AMOUNT
BUDGET:	TOTAL:

SAVED	AMOUNT
BUDGET:	TOTAL:

EXPENSES	AMOUNT
BUDGET:	TOTAL:

Weekly **PROGRESS**

WEEK OF

	GOAL	ACTUAL	DIFFERENCE + / -
EARNED			
SPENT			
SAVED			
DEBT			

INCOME	AMOUNT
BUDGET:	**TOTAL:**

EXPENSES	AMOUNT
BUDGET:	**TOTAL:**

SAVED	AMOUNT
BUDGET:	**TOTAL:**

Weekly PROGRESS

WEEK OF

	GOAL	ACTUAL	DIFFERENCE + / -
EARNED			
SPENT			
SAVED			
DEBT			

INCOME	AMOUNT
BUDGET:	TOTAL:

SAVED	AMOUNT
BUDGET:	TOTAL:

EXPENSES	AMOUNT
BUDGET:	TOTAL:

Weekly **PROGRESS**

WEEK OF

	GOAL	ACTUAL	DIFFERENCE + / -
EARNED			
SPENT			
SAVED			
DEBT			

INCOME	AMOUNT
BUDGET:	**TOTAL:**

EXPENSES	AMOUNT
BUDGET:	**TOTAL:**

SAVED	AMOUNT
BUDGET:	**TOTAL:**

MONDAY	TUESDAY	WEDNESDAY	THURSDAY

MONTH AT A GLANCE

FRIDAY	SATURDAY	SUNDAY	NOTES

Budget OVERVIEW

MONTH

UTILITIES	BUDGET	SPENT

PERSONAL	BUDGET	SPENT

HOME	BUDGET	SPENT

TRASPORTATION	BUDGET	SPENT

FOOD / DRINKS	BUDGET	SPENT

MEDICAL	BUDGET	SPENT

GIVING	BUDGET	SPENT

DEBTS	BUDGET	SPENT

INCOME	AMOUNT	DATE

OTHER	START	FINISH

WEEK OF

	GOAL	ACTUAL	DIFFERENCE + / -
EARNED			
SPENT			
SAVED			
DEBT			

INCOME	AMOUNT
BUDGET:	TOTAL:

EXPENSES	AMOUNT
BUDGET:	TOTAL:

SAVED	AMOUNT
BUDGET:	TOTAL:

Weekly **PROGRESS**

WEEK OF

	GOAL	ACTUAL	DIFFERENCE + / -
EARNED			
SPENT			
SAVED			
DEBT			

INCOME	AMOUNT
BUDGET:	TOTAL:

EXPENSES	AMOUNT
BUDGET:	TOTAL:

SAVED	AMOUNT
BUDGET:	TOTAL:

Weekly **PROGRESS**

WEEK OF

	GOAL	ACTUAL	DIFFERENCE + / -
EARNED			
SPENT			
SAVED			
DEBT			

INCOME	AMOUNT
BUDGET:	TOTAL:

EXPENSES	AMOUNT
BUDGET:	TOTAL:

SAVED	AMOUNT
BUDGET:	TOTAL:

Weekly PROGRESS

	GOAL	ACTUAL	DIFFERENCE + / -
EARNED			
SPENT			
SAVED			
DEBT			

INCOME	AMOUNT
BUDGET:	TOTAL:

EXPENSES	AMOUNT
BUDGET:	TOTAL:

SAVED	AMOUNT
BUDGET:	TOTAL:

Weekly **PROGRESS**

WEEK OF

	GOAL	ACTUAL	DIFFERENCE + / -
EARNED			
SPENT			
SAVED			
DEBT			

INCOME	AMOUNT
BUDGET:	TOTAL:

SAVED	AMOUNT
BUDGET:	TOTAL:

EXPENSES	AMOUNT
BUDGET:	TOTAL:

MONDAY	TUESDAY	WEDNESDAY	THURSDAY

FRIDAY	SATURDAY	SUNDAY	NOTES

Budget OVERVIEW

UTILITIES	BUDGET	SPENT

PERSONAL	BUDGET	SPENT

HOME	BUDGET	SPENT

TRASPORTATION	BUDGET	SPENT

FOOD / DRINKS	BUDGET	SPENT

MEDICAL	BUDGET	SPENT

GIVING	BUDGET	SPENT

DEBTS	BUDGET	SPENT

INCOME	AMOUNT	DATE

OTHER	START	FINISH

Weekly **PROGRESS**

WEEK OF

	GOAL	ACTUAL	DIFFERENCE + / -
EARNED			
SPENT			
SAVED			
DEBT			

INCOME	AMOUNT
BUDGET:	TOTAL:

SAVED	AMOUNT
BUDGET:	TOTAL:

EXPENSES	AMOUNT
BUDGET:	TOTAL:

Weekly PROGRESS

WEEK OF

	GOAL	ACTUAL	DIFFERENCE +/-
EARNED			
SPENT			
SAVED			
DEBT			

INCOME	AMOUNT
BUDGET:	TOTAL:

EXPENSES	AMOUNT
BUDGET:	TOTAL:

SAVED	AMOUNT
BUDGET:	TOTAL:

Weekly **PROGRESS**

WEEK OF

	GOAL	ACTUAL	DIFFERENCE + / -
EARNED			
SPENT			
SAVED			
DEBT			

INCOME	AMOUNT
BUDGET:	**TOTAL:**

SAVED	AMOUNT
BUDGET:	**TOTAL:**

EXPENSES	AMOUNT
BUDGET:	**TOTAL:**

Weekly PROGRESS

WEEK OF

	GOAL	ACTUAL	DIFFERENCE + / -
EARNED			
SPENT			
SAVED			
DEBT			

INCOME	AMOUNT
BUDGET:	TOTAL:

SAVED	AMOUNT
BUDGET:	TOTAL:

EXPENSES	AMOUNT
BUDGET:	TOTAL:

Weekly **PROGRESS**

WEEK OF

	GOAL	ACTUAL	DIFFERENCE + / -
EARNED			
SPENT			
SAVED			
DEBT			

INCOME	AMOUNT
BUDGET:	TOTAL:

SAVED	AMOUNT
BUDGET:	TOTAL:

EXPENSES	AMOUNT
BUDGET:	TOTAL:

MONDAY	TUESDAY	WEDNESDAY	THURSDAY

FRIDAY	SATURDAY	SUNDAY	NOTES

Budget OVERVIEW

UTILITIES	BUDGET	SPENT

PERSONAL	BUDGET	SPENT

HOME	BUDGET	SPENT

TRASPORTATION	BUDGET	SPENT

FOOD / DRINKS	BUDGET	SPENT

MEDICAL	BUDGET	SPENT

GIVING	BUDGET	SPENT

DEBTS	BUDGET	SPENT

INCOME	AMOUNT	DATE

OTHER	START	FINISH

Weekly PROGRESS

WEEK OF

	GOAL	ACTUAL	DIFFERENCE + / -
EARNED			
SPENT			
SAVED			
DEBT			

INCOME	AMOUNT
BUDGET:	TOTAL:

SAVED	AMOUNT
BUDGET:	TOTAL:

EXPENSES	AMOUNT
BUDGET:	TOTAL:

Weekly **PROGRESS**

WEEK OF

	GOAL	ACTUAL	DIFFERENCE + / -
EARNED			
SPENT			
SAVED			
DEBT			

INCOME	AMOUNT
BUDGET:	TOTAL:

SAVED	AMOUNT
BUDGET:	TOTAL:

EXPENSES	AMOUNT
BUDGET:	TOTAL:

Weekly **PROGRESS**

WEEK OF

	GOAL	ACTUAL	DIFFERENCE + / -
EARNED			
SPENT			
SAVED			
DEBT			

INCOME	AMOUNT
BUDGET:	**TOTAL:**

SAVED	AMOUNT
BUDGET:	**TOTAL:**

EXPENSES	AMOUNT
BUDGET:	**TOTAL:**

Weekly **PROGRESS**

WEEK OF

	GOAL	ACTUAL	DIFFERENCE + / -
EARNED			
SPENT			
SAVED			
DEBT			

INCOME	AMOUNT
BUDGET:	TOTAL:

EXPENSES	AMOUNT
BUDGET:	TOTAL:

SAVED	AMOUNT
BUDGET:	TOTAL:

Weekly **PROGRESS**

WEEK OF

	GOAL	ACTUAL	DIFFERENCE + / -
EARNED			
SPENT			
SAVED			
DEBT			

INCOME	AMOUNT
BUDGET:	TOTAL:

SAVED	AMOUNT
BUDGET:	TOTAL:

EXPENSES	AMOUNT
BUDGET:	TOTAL:

MONDAY	TUESDAY	WEDNESDAY	THURSDAY

FRIDAY	SATURDAY	SUNDAY	NOTES

Budget **OVERVIEW**

MONTH

UTILITIES	BUDGET	SPENT

PERSONAL	BUDGET	SPENT

HOME	BUDGET	SPENT

TRASPORTATION	BUDGET	SPENT

FOOD / DRINKS	BUDGET	SPENT

MEDICAL	BUDGET	SPENT

GIVING	BUDGET	SPENT

DEBTS	BUDGET	SPENT

INCOME	AMOUNT	DATE

OTHER	START	FINISH

Weekly **PROGRESS**

WEEK OF

	GOAL	ACTUAL	DIFFERENCE + / -
EARNED			
SPENT			
SAVED			
DEBT			

INCOME	AMOUNT	EXPENSES	AMOUNT
BUDGET:	TOTAL:		

SAVED	AMOUNT
BUDGET:	TOTAL:

EXPENSES	AMOUNT
BUDGET:	TOTAL:

Weekly **PROGRESS**

WEEK OF

	GOAL	ACTUAL	DIFFERENCE + / -
EARNED			
SPENT			
SAVED			
DEBT			

INCOME	AMOUNT
BUDGET:	TOTAL:

SAVED	AMOUNT
BUDGET:	TOTAL:

EXPENSES	AMOUNT
BUDGET:	TOTAL:

Weekly PROGRESS

WEEK OF

	GOAL	ACTUAL	DIFFERENCE + / -
EARNED			
SPENT			
SAVED			
DEBT			

INCOME	AMOUNT
BUDGET:	TOTAL:

EXPENSES	AMOUNT
BUDGET:	TOTAL:

SAVED	AMOUNT
BUDGET:	TOTAL:

Weekly PROGRESS

WEEK OF

	GOAL	ACTUAL	DIFFERENCE + / -
EARNED			
SPENT			
SAVED			
DEBT			

INCOME	AMOUNT
BUDGET:	TOTAL:

EXPENSES	AMOUNT
BUDGET:	TOTAL:

SAVED	AMOUNT
BUDGET:	TOTAL:

Weekly **PROGRESS**

WEEK OF

	GOAL	ACTUAL	DIFFERENCE + / -
EARNED			
SPENT			
SAVED			
DEBT			

INCOME	AMOUNT
BUDGET:	TOTAL:

EXPENSES	AMOUNT
BUDGET:	TOTAL:

SAVED	AMOUNT
BUDGET:	TOTAL:

MONDAY	TUESDAY	WEDNESDAY	THURSDAY

FRIDAY	SATURDAY	SUNDAY	NOTES

Budget OVERVIEW

UTILITIES	BUDGET	SPENT

PERSONAL	BUDGET	SPENT

HOME	BUDGET	SPENT

TRASPORTATION	BUDGET	SPENT

FOOD / DRINKS	BUDGET	SPENT

MEDICAL	BUDGET	SPENT

GIVING	BUDGET	SPENT

DEBTS	BUDGET	SPENT

INCOME	AMOUNT	DATE

OTHER	START	FINISH

Weekly **PROGRESS**

	WEEK OF

	GOAL	ACTUAL	DIFFERENCE + / -
EARNED			
SPENT			
SAVED			
DEBT			

INCOME	AMOUNT
BUDGET:	TOTAL:

EXPENSES	AMOUNT
BUDGET:	TOTAL:

SAVED	AMOUNT
BUDGET:	TOTAL:

Weekly PROGRESS

WEEK OF

	GOAL	ACTUAL	DIFFERENCE + / -
EARNED			
SPENT			
SAVED			
DEBT			

INCOME	AMOUNT
BUDGET:	TOTAL:

SAVED	AMOUNT
BUDGET:	TOTAL:

EXPENSES	AMOUNT
BUDGET:	TOTAL:

Weekly **PROGRESS**

	WEEK OF

	GOAL	ACTUAL	DIFFERENCE + / -
EARNED			
SPENT			
SAVED			
DEBT			

INCOME	AMOUNT
BUDGET:	**TOTAL:**

SAVED	AMOUNT
BUDGET:	**TOTAL:**

EXPENSES	AMOUNT
BUDGET:	**TOTAL:**

Weekly PROGRESS

WEEK OF

	GOAL	ACTUAL	DIFFERENCE + / -
EARNED			
SPENT			
SAVED			
DEBT			

INCOME	AMOUNT
BUDGET:	TOTAL:

SAVED	AMOUNT
BUDGET:	TOTAL:

EXPENSES	AMOUNT
BUDGET:	TOTAL:

Weekly PROGRESS

WEEK OF

	GOAL	ACTUAL	DIFFERENCE + / -
EARNED			
SPENT			
SAVED			
DEBT			

INCOME		AMOUNT
BUDGET:		**TOTAL:**

EXPENSES		AMOUNT
BUDGET:		**TOTAL:**

SAVED		AMOUNT
BUDGET:		**TOTAL:**

MONDAY	TUESDAY	WEDNESDAY	THURSDAY

FRIDAY	SATURDAY	SUNDAY	NOTES

Budget OVERVIEW

UTILITIES	BUDGET	SPENT

PERSONAL	BUDGET	SPENT

HOME	BUDGET	SPENT

TRASPORTATION	BUDGET	SPENT

FOOD / DRINKS	BUDGET	SPENT

MEDICAL	BUDGET	SPENT

GIVING	BUDGET	SPENT

DEBTS	BUDGET	SPENT

INCOME	AMOUNT	DATE

OTHER	START	FINISH

Weekly **PROGRESS**

WEEK OF

	GOAL	ACTUAL	DIFFERENCE + / -
EARNED			
SPENT			
SAVED			
DEBT			

INCOME	AMOUNT
BUDGET:	**TOTAL:**

SAVED	AMOUNT
BUDGET:	**TOTAL:**

EXPENSES	AMOUNT
BUDGET:	**TOTAL:**

Weekly **PROGRESS**

WEEK OF

	GOAL	ACTUAL	DIFFERENCE + / -
EARNED			
SPENT			
SAVED			
DEBT			

INCOME	AMOUNT
BUDGET:	TOTAL:

EXPENSES	AMOUNT
BUDGET:	TOTAL:

SAVED	AMOUNT
BUDGET:	TOTAL:

Weekly **PROGRESS**

WEEK OF

	GOAL	ACTUAL	DIFFERENCE + / -
EARNED			
SPENT			
SAVED			
DEBT			

INCOME	AMOUNT
BUDGET:	TOTAL:

EXPENSES	AMOUNT
BUDGET:	TOTAL:

SAVED	AMOUNT
BUDGET:	TOTAL:

Weekly **PROGRESS**

WEEK OF

	GOAL	ACTUAL	DIFFERENCE + / -
EARNED			
SPENT			
SAVED			
DEBT			

INCOME	AMOUNT
BUDGET:	TOTAL:

SAVED	AMOUNT
BUDGET:	TOTAL:

EXPENSES	AMOUNT
BUDGET:	TOTAL:

Weekly PROGRESS

WEEK OF

	GOAL	ACTUAL	DIFFERENCE + / -
EARNED			
SPENT			
SAVED			
DEBT			

INCOME	AMOUNT
BUDGET:	TOTAL:

EXPENSES	AMOUNT
BUDGET:	TOTAL:

SAVED	AMOUNT
BUDGET:	TOTAL:

MONDAY	TUESDAY	WEDNESDAY	THURSDAY

FRIDAY	SATURDAY	SUNDAY	NOTES

Budget **OVERVIEW**

MONTH

UTILITIES	BUDGET	SPENT

PERSONAL	BUDGET	SPENT

HOME	BUDGET	SPENT

TRASPORTATION	BUDGET	SPENT

FOOD / DRINKS	BUDGET	SPENT

MEDICAL	BUDGET	SPENT

GIVING	BUDGET	SPENT

DEBTS	BUDGET	SPENT

INCOME	AMOUNT	DATE

OTHER	START	FINISH

Weekly **PROGRESS**

WEEK OF

	GOAL	ACTUAL	DIFFERENCE + / -
EARNED			
SPENT			
SAVED			
DEBT			

INCOME	AMOUNT
BUDGET:	TOTAL:

SAVED	AMOUNT
BUDGET:	TOTAL:

EXPENSES	AMOUNT
BUDGET:	TOTAL:

Weekly **PROGRESS**

WEEK OF

	GOAL	ACTUAL	DIFFERENCE +/-
EARNED			
SPENT			
SAVED			
DEBT			

INCOME	AMOUNT
BUDGET:	**TOTAL:**

SAVED	AMOUNT
BUDGET:	**TOTAL:**

EXPENSES	AMOUNT
BUDGET:	**TOTAL:**

Weekly **PROGRESS**

WEEK OF

	GOAL	ACTUAL	DIFFERENCE + / -
EARNED			
SPENT			
SAVED			
DEBT			

INCOME	AMOUNT
BUDGET:	TOTAL:

SAVED	AMOUNT
BUDGET:	TOTAL:

EXPENSES	AMOUNT
BUDGET:	TOTAL:

Weekly **PROGRESS**

WEEK OF

	GOAL	ACTUAL	DIFFERENCE + / -
EARNED			
SPENT			
SAVED			
DEBT			

INCOME	AMOUNT
BUDGET:	TOTAL:

EXPENSES	AMOUNT
BUDGET:	TOTAL:

SAVED	AMOUNT
BUDGET:	TOTAL:

Weekly **PROGRESS**

WEEK OF

	GOAL	ACTUAL	DIFFERENCE + / -
EARNED			
SPENT			
SAVED			
DEBT			

INCOME	AMOUNT	EXPENSES	AMOUNT
BUDGET:	TOTAL:		

SAVED	AMOUNT
BUDGET:	TOTAL:

EXPENSES (cont.)	AMOUNT
BUDGET:	TOTAL:

MONDAY	TUESDAY	WEDNESDAY	THURSDAY

FRIDAY	SATURDAY	SUNDAY	NOTES

Budget OVERVIEW

MONTH

UTILITIES	BUDGET	SPENT

PERSONAL	BUDGET	SPENT

HOME	BUDGET	SPENT

TRASPORTATION	BUDGET	SPENT

FOOD / DRINKS	BUDGET	SPENT

MEDICAL	BUDGET	SPENT

GIVING	BUDGET	SPENT

DEBTS	BUDGET	SPENT

INCOME	AMOUNT	DATE

OTHER	START	FINISH

Weekly **PROGRESS**

WEEK OF

	GOAL	ACTUAL	DIFFERENCE + / -
EARNED			
SPENT			
SAVED			
DEBT			

INCOME	AMOUNT
BUDGET:	**TOTAL:**

SAVED	AMOUNT
BUDGET:	**TOTAL:**

EXPENSES	AMOUNT
BUDGET:	**TOTAL:**

Weekly PROGRESS

WEEK OF

	GOAL	ACTUAL	DIFFERENCE + / -
EARNED			
SPENT			
SAVED			
DEBT			

INCOME	AMOUNT
BUDGET:	TOTAL:

EXPENSES	AMOUNT
BUDGET:	TOTAL:

SAVED	AMOUNT
BUDGET:	TOTAL:

Weekly PROGRESS

WEEK OF

	GOAL	ACTUAL	DIFFERENCE + / -
EARNED			
SPENT			
SAVED			
DEBT			

INCOME	AMOUNT
BUDGET:	TOTAL:

SAVED	AMOUNT
BUDGET:	TOTAL:

EXPENSES	AMOUNT
BUDGET:	TOTAL:

Weekly **PROGRESS**

WEEK OF

	GOAL	ACTUAL	DIFFERENCE + / -
EARNED			
SPENT			
SAVED			
DEBT			

INCOME	AMOUNT
BUDGET:	TOTAL:

SAVED	AMOUNT
BUDGET:	TOTAL:

EXPENSES	AMOUNT
BUDGET:	TOTAL:

Weekly **PROGRESS**

WEEK OF

	GOAL	ACTUAL	DIFFERENCE + / -
EARNED			
SPENT			
SAVED			
DEBT			

INCOME	AMOUNT
BUDGET:	TOTAL:

SAVED	AMOUNT
BUDGET:	TOTAL:

EXPENSES	AMOUNT
BUDGET:	TOTAL:

Monthly Expense END OF THE YEAR

| INCOME | EXPENSES | DIFFERENCE |

HOUSING EXPENSES

RENT/MORTGAGE

TAXES

TOTAL

TRANSPORTATION COSTS

CAR PAYMENT

INSURANCE

GAS

TOTAL

MEDICAL & DENTAL EXPENSES

MEDICATION

TOTAL

OTHER EXPENSES

CREDIT CARD

CREDIT CARD

TOTAL

UTILITIES & HOUSEHOLD BILLS

GAS

ELECTRIC

WATER

INTERNET/CABLE

SUBSCRIPTIONS

PHONE

TOTAL

FOOD & GROCERY

GROCERY

DINING OUT

TOTAL

PERSONAL EXPENSES

CLOTHING

ENTERTAIMENT

OTHER

OTHER

OTHER

TOTAL

TOTAL MONTHLY EXPENSES

Printed in Great Britain
by Amazon